FRAGILE HANDLE WITH CARE.

A woman's journey to finding love

Copyright © 2019

All rights reserved. No part of this book may be reproduced in any form on by an electronic or mechanical means, including information storage and retrieval systems, without permission in writing from the author, except by a reviewer who may quote brief passages in a review.

TABLE OF CONTENTS

A BOY, NOT A MAN 1

FIXED FIGHT 3

A WALL 6

LITTLE MISS GOODIE TWO SHOES 8

BAG LADY 11

BEAUTIFUL CHAOS 13

BLACK SHEEP 16

DADDY ISSUES 19

DON'T QUIT 23

THE FROG AND THE PRINCE 27

I AM NOT..29

I CHOOSE TO LOVE 32

I WISH...35

I WOULD BE LYING 38

IF YOU 41

I'M NOT HIM..43

ME 47

MY TRUE LOVE 49

LEAGUE OF MY OWN 52

THANK YOU 55

TOO MUCH SAUCE 60

TORN 63

WHY ME 66

BUT I'M WORKING ON IT 69

YOU DESERVE IT..72

A BOY, NOT A MAN

1 COR 13:11

FRAGILE, HANDLE WITH CARE.

A BOY NOT A MAN

Stop giving him a title he don't live up to.
You call him a man, but he can't fit those shoes.
He says he loves you, but that is not true.
But you still hold him down, where they do that boo.
He beats you down, but you forgive that too.
He sleeps around and says he's tired of you.
And if you mention a job, he says he's bleeding the block.
 Instead of hitting on you, he needs to punch that clock.
He says, "I'm a man and I'm going to do me."
But he's not doing shit as far as I can see.
He's playing you like he play those games,
yet you're tolerating it. So whose really to blame?
Sister, realize that you deserve better.
Some flowers, some candy, a simple love letter.
Some "Thank you baby for holding me down."
Some "I love you for always sticking around."
Some "I got all the bills. Go ahead and spend your check.
Pamper yourself let me massage YOUR neck.
Prop your legs up here. Let me massage YOUR feet.
Let me fix YOUR plate. The queen has to eat."
So, if he's NOT doing these things you must understand.
You're dealing with a boy... not a man.

1 COR 13:11

FIXED FIGHT

2 CHRONICLES 20:15

FIXED FIGHT

Some say I can rap.
Some say I'm a poet.
But I'm a child of GOD,
and it's my job to show it.

Actions speak louder than words,
or haven't you heard
That faith comes by hearing the word.

Some say I'm a writer by the things I write.
I choose to walk by faith, and not by sight.

Often times, I ask myself
what do they see that I don't.
Maybe it's something deep within,
maybe it's the God in me.

Some say I'm perfect,
but I don't know why.
I'm just a sinner, saved by grace,
the Apple of his eyes.

I'm just a vessel willing to be used.
hurt by the world and love abused,
Broken by pain but my many scars don't show.
I raise my head, wipe my tears, and off I go.

Yes, I know that the battle is not mine,
yet it seems like I'm battling ALL the time.

But it's ok. I know I will be alright.
Because I also heard
This is a fixed fight.

2 CHRONICLES 20:15

A WALL

PSALMS 147:3

FRAGILE, HANDLE WITH CARE.

A WALL

She was hurt by love, so she's a bit standoffish.
Some call her boujee while others call her selfish.

They say she walks around with her nose in the air.
Her beauty is captivating, so one can't help but stare.

Every time you see her she has a smile on her face.
She speaks with excellence, walks with grace.

But behind her smile, she sheds many tears.
She's broken and been that way for years.

Sometimes, a smile can hide what the heart doesn't show.
Sometimes, the hurt is deeper than you know.

So, she keeps to herself. She's in her own little world.
Outside she's a grown woman, but inside she's a hurt little girl.

She hides the pain that was caused by loving the wrong man.
She keeps it to herself. Nobody would understand.

But best believe, if you need her, she's at your beck and call.
She will heal one day,
but until then she hides her hurt behind
a wall.
PSALMS 147:3

LITTLE MISS GOODIE TWO SHOES

PROVERBS 31

LITTLE MISS GOODIE TWO SHOES

Growing up she was labeled Miss Goodie Two Shoes
because she didn't do what others use to do.

She grew up drinking tea and eating crumpets.
Her friends played the flute, the clarinet.
Her choice was the trumpet.

She was constantly teased for being different and kind of strange,
but she didn't care about it in a world that was all the same,

In a world filled with pretty dresses and pretty little pink bows.
Cut off shorts, tank tops, and socks filled with holes.

Skipping rocks across the lake brought her joy.
She was catching lizards and chasing frogs while her friends were chasing boys.

She was treated as an outcast, some rare form of disease.
So every night, she would cry herself to sleep.

She'd often wonder why she wasn't like the others.
She was ok being alone or just playing with her brothers.

She knew that little town could not hold her big dreams,
so she vowed to get out, get out by any means.

At least she would be far away from all the looks and stares.
She could wear baseball caps instead of fixing hair.

But to her dismay, she encountered the same sort of things.

Because, at her work office, they gave her the same ole name,
Little Miss Goodie Two Shoes..
MORAL: It's ok to be different. You decide who you want to be and let others decide if they want to be part of who you are or not, either way.... YOU BE YOU... The world needs your differenve.

Proverbs 31

BAG LADY:

1 PETER 5:7

BAG LADY

She walks around with baggage from the past.

Bags of broken relationships that she thought would last,
bags of insecurities making her constantly ask why,
and all the tears she shed have formed bags under her eyes.

Several bags of pain.
So many bags of regret.
She often tells herself
this is as good as it gets.

So, she continues lugging around all that heavy weight,
praying for relief, for a break.

Bag Lady,
Keep the faith.
It will be ok.

Cast all your cares on God.
He will make a way.

You haven't let go of the past
if you're still carrying the hurt with you.

1 PETER 5:7

BEAUTIFUL CHAOS:

PSALMS 139:14

BEAUTIFUL CHAOS

She was hurt by love,
so she's a little skeptical.
Sexually abused,
so she's a bit nonsexual.
Verbally abused,
so she doesn't say much.
Often times, you see her shying away from a touch.

Physically abused from speaking her mind.
so her silence speaks volumes,
most of the time.

But with the right man,
you just might get a smile,
especially if she likes your style.

Even though she knows laughter is good for the soul,
when things start to heat up, she instantly turns cold.

She walks around as if nothing is wrong,
twirling her hair, singing her song.

She's in her own zone, company of one.
Though broken inside, she still has fun.

She's to herself, keeps everyone out her business.

FRAGILE, HANDLE WITH CARE.

She's fine as heck, and the Lord's my witness.
And if you push her too much, best believe she's going to box (LOL).
So, I gave her the name
Beautiful Chaos.

PSALMS 34:18

BLACK SHEEP:
PSALMS 139:14

BLACK SHEEP

Yes, you're different,
God made you that way,
Black Sheep.

Yes, you're the outcast,
God made you that way,
Black Sheep.

Yes, they treat you funny, but it's ok.
Laughter is good for the soul,
Black Sheep.

I know it hurts,
but God is a healer,
Black Sheep.

I know it's not right,
but God will correct it,
Black Sheep.

They think you're weak,
but God knows your stronger,
Black Sheep.

They cast you aside,
but God says I got you,
Black Sheep.

Everybody sees you
in the midst of the white sheep.
You were created to stand out!!!

PSALMS 139:14

DADDY ISSUES

HEB 13:5

DADDY ISSUES

So, she often found herself choosing the wrong man,
Going from broken relationship after broken relationship
but never fully understanding

Why she's mentally and physically abused,
beaten, battered, broken
and constantly being used.

She gave herself away
to every Tom, Dick and Harry.
When they didn't fulfill her needs,
she called up her friend, Mary.

She had a very strong sensual and sexual appetite.
Her hunger to be loved and to be accepted
were in a constant fight.

She drank lots of liquor.
She smoked a lot of weed.
When those didn't do the trick,
her plug introduced her to speed,

Which lead to tooting powder and experimenting with X.
When she didn't have the money for her fix,
she paid the plug with sex,
all a part of his devilish plan.

FRAGILE, HANDLE WITH CARE.

She didn't have to pay for her drugs,
because the plug was now her man.
She got high as a kite and got her high for free.
(so she thought).

She felt being high everyday
was the only way to be.

One day,
while riding with her man to make a drop,
oh boy ran a red light and was pulled over by a cop.

They were told to get out and put their hands on the hood.
He said he was going to have to search the car and asked permission
if he could.

Long story short,
she's now doing five to ten.
He visits her every other Saturday,
sends her money for paper and pens.

One day during visitation,
she had this awkward face.
He asked, "Are you ok, babe?"
She replied, "Why didn't you take the case?"

"Because I'm a two-time loser,
and one more would be my third strike.

So, I had to tell him the drugs were yours.

You're young.
It's your first time. You will be alright."

He told her that he loved her
and then blew her a kiss.
She blew one back
and said, "I love you too. We will get thru this."

So she turned her back,
ready to walk back to her dorm.
She turned to look one last time
only to see another on his arm...

HEB 13:5

DON'T QUIT

PROVERBS 31

DON T QUIT

Don't quit. You're almost there.
Keep pushing thru all your fears.

Though you can't see through the tears,
my God says
This is your year.

The many trials you've been through,
they thought they would discourage you.
You kept on going. You made it thru.
When you were weak, I carried you.

Don't quit, and here's the reason.
It's your time. It's your season.

Satan thought he had you,
thought he had you bound.

You pressed on.
Look at you now.
For all your struggles,
here's your crown.

Don't quit,
for I am here with you.
I know all the struggles you've been thru.

And when you didn't know what to do,
You kept on praying,

I'm proud of you.
You've done well,
I always knew you would.

You have done exactly what you should.
You trusted me thru it all.
Those storms of life didn't make you fall.

You didn't quit.
You stayed strong and stood tall.

For me, my child,
you endured it all.

I'm so glad you answered the call.
No longer Saul, I call you Paul.
There is power in my name.
You spoke it boldly
You weren't ashamed.
The name above every name,
Jesus!!!

Don't quit.
And after all is said and done,

I call you daughter. I call you son.

For the victory, you have won,
and I can say it is done.

Because you didn't quit,
this is a song God put in my spirit
For the body of Christ
who has pushed thru things
that Satan assigned to destroy them.

God says
Well done,
my good and faithful servants.

Now enjoy the spoils from your victory,
I am Samuel,
but Jesus is Lord.

Good morning.

Proverbs 31

THE FROG AND THE PRINCE:

PROVERBS 31

THE FROG AND THE PRINCE

Ladies,
know how to recognize
the frog from the prince.

Just because the turtle was slower than the hare
doesn't mean you have to wait on his #ss.

Stop basing your relationship
on Jack and his beanstalk.

Because at the end of that rainbow
is not the goose that laid the golden egg
or a pot of gold for that matter.

And please
Stop taking care of him and his 7 Lil Dwarfs
unless he's bringing home some
jolly green giants lol.

Do not allow him to bring home the Three Little Pigs (homies),
Who will eat you out of a house and home
And have you looking like Old Mother Hubbard.

To sum it all up,
Stop believing in his
fairytales....
Proverbs 31

I AM NOT:

PROVERBS 31

I AM NOT

I am not your child,
so this yelling must cease.

Instead of being my storm,
can you be my peace?

I am not your punching bag,
so please keep your hands off me.

I am not your door mat
where you wipe your feet.

I am not someone
you take advantage of.
I'm supposed to be
the one you claim to love.

I am not your wash cloth
you use to wash your tail.

Why do I give you heaven
when all you give me is hell?

I am not a grudge
you hold on to from your past.

FRAGILE, HANDLE WITH CARE.

I am your forever,
someone built to last.

I refuse to be your trash can
where you dump your trash into.

Though you constantly hurt me,
I continue to love you.

I am not begging you to stay.
You have the option to leave,
but I also am not going to let you
come and go as you please.

So, if you decide to stay,
I am not putting up with this.
And if this continues,
you will not be missed.

I am love and love
is me.

Proverbs 31

I CHOOSE TO LOVE:

PROVERBS 31

I CHOOSE TO LOVE

I choose to love in a world filled with hate.
I choose to pray as I wait
for circumstances to change for the better.
I choose not to leave. Let's stay together.

I choose to speak up on racism
and not to judge by the color of someone's skin.
I choose to always represent myself as a man
though society treats me like a dog in this foreign land.

I choose to treat a woman like a queen,
to take her to places she hasn't seen.
I choose to respect even when it is not given,
I choose to enjoy this life I'm living.

I choose to smile even with tears in my eyes.
People are so hateful, but I know not why.

I choose to help someone in their time of need.
I choose to remember I'm Abraham's seed,
a child of the Most High
who calls me the apple of His eye.

I choose to honor Rosa, Mandela, Martin Luther King,
knowing I come from greatness. I too am a king.
I choose to remember it made me who I am today,
that I've learned and grown from all my mistakes.

I choose to stand up, speak up.
I do have a voice.
I choose to be me,
Why? Because it's my choice.

In this life, you may win. You may lose.
But it doesn't matter.
It's what you choose.

Proverbs 31

I WISH:
PROVERBS 31

I WISH

I wish I could take the pain away
you encountered throughout the years.

I wish I could help you
wipe away the tears.

I wish I could help you
get past your fears.

I wish I could whisper sweet nothing
in your ears.

Like God loves you,
He sees all your struggles.
He sees the heart
men have broken.

He knows the mistakes you made,
yet He understands.

I wish I could hold you
and let you cry in my arms.
I wish they could help keep you warm
from a world that's been so cold.

Above all,
I wish and I know

God will heal your soul.

I wish you love
For God is love.

Proverbs 31

I WOULD BE LYING:

PROVERBS 31

I WOULD BE LYING

If I said I don't miss you,
Or miss kissing you,
Or I don't think about you,
Or I don't care for you.

I would be lying
if I said it doesn't hurt.
but I understand, for what it's worth.

God's plans for us were different
from what we had in mind.
Just know that I think about you all the time,

What you're doing,
who's loving you,
Who are texting, who's calling,
who's making love to you,

Who's taking you to movies,
who's buying you popcorn,
Who's buying you juju bees and candy corn.

I would be lying
if I said I catch myself staring into space.
As I close my eyes,
I see your face.

I would be lying
if I said I don't wish the best for you.

But I'm ok with it all,
and that's the truth.

I'm in a better place,
I've learned to love me.
Because in losing you,
I found me.

Proverbs 31

IF YOU

If you allow me to love you,
I promise I won't hurt you.
I need you to trust me.

I know you've been hurt,
let down,
beaten by people
who didn't know how to love.

Come here.
Let me hold you.
Rest your head on my shoulder. Relax.

Let it go.
Let go of all the pain,
all the broken promises.
all the anger,
all the deceit.

Let it all go.
Now allow mw to show me
What love truly is.

Proverbs 31

I'M NOT HIM:

PROVERBS 31

I M NOT HIM

Mom, can we talk?

>'Bout what? I'm busy.

Why don't you love me?

>Here we go,
>I bore you,
>I got to love you.

But why we can't get along?
What did I do so bad
for you not to love me,
to want to spend time with me?

Are you ashamed of me?
You treat my other siblings so much better.

>Sit, dear child.

>A product of love you were not.
>You were a product of rape,
>so I'm giving you all I've got.

>You see, I was abused mentally and physically
>by your father,
>and in that abuse, I bore a daughter.

FRAGILE, HANDLE WITH CARE.

        I tried to abort you,
        but he wasn't having it.

      He threatened to kill me, my family,
         and I believed him.

       I was beaten, kicked, punched,
      wore glasses because of black eyes.
        I was totally humiliated,
         and I don't know why.

       He cheated on me constantly,
       even with family and friends.
    It seemed, at times, that this hurt had no end.

        Yes, I tried to get away,
         many many times,
     but this man had my body and my mind.

        And every time I see you,
        I see this got damn man.

         I want to love you,
        but can't you understand?

         You walk like him,
          talk like him,

act like him too,

and this is why it's hard for me to love you.

But I'm not him.

Proverbs 31

ME

PROVERBS 31

ME

Most tears I shed,
I shed alone.
When I hurt,
I hurt on my own.

The pain I feel
hurts like hell.
I just hold my head up
and say, "Oh well."

We all have our cross to bear,
even when life isn't fair.
Life will have its ups and downs.
It's not all smiles, sometimes frowns.

I can't help how I feel.
All's I know is that I am real.

So, sorry, if I don't do like you think,
but I will stand tall.
You can take that to the bank.

So never feel sorry
about what you may see.
I'm not perfect.
I'm not flawless.

I'm just me.
Proverbs 31

MY TRUE LOVE

PROVERBS 31

MY TRUE LOVE

If you can see you thru my eyes.
I'm pretty sure you'll realize
how truly special your really are
my guiding light and shining star.

I know the world has let you down,
that the love you've searched for
has not been found,

How you've given your heart away
countless times.
only to receive heartbreak
time after time.

But you can trust your heart with me.

I'll take care of it,
just trust me.
I know you're taking a chance again.

I want to be more
than just your friend.
I'm here to tear down those walls.
I am at your beck and call.
And if by chance you might fall,
I'm right there thru it all.

Those tears you've shed from other guys,
I'll gently wipe them from your eyes.
And after all is said and done,
I hope you realize I am the one
Who has loved you all your life.

I now know the meaning of love at first sight.
For I have loved you since the very first day.

I lift you up in prayer constantly.
Yes, my love, I pray for you.
That's what a man is supposed to do.

So, I'll end this with
"See you soon, my love,"
and continue to pray to God up above.

For my future wife,
my true love.

Proverbs 31

LEAGUE OF MY OWN

PROVERBS 31

LEAGUE OF MY OWN

I approached her,
and she said,
"I think I'm out your league."

I smiled and replied,
"It's ok. For you, I'll make an exception."

She smiled and said,
"No, you must not have heard or misunderstood me,
I said I'm out your league. "

I said, "No,
I heard and understood you just fine.
The fact of the matter is,
I'm in my own league.

You see society has a way of categorizing us,
hence the reason you said league.

We are categorized by race, gender,
the haves, the have nots,
the rich, the poor, so on and so forth.

So, I decided
I didn't want to be categorized
just be me and form my own league.

The only requirement
is you be yourself.

I don't care
what ethnicity you are,
how much money you have or don't.

I don't care as long as you're happy,
honest,
treat people correctly,
and just be you.

So, she smiled,
batted her eyes,
and proceeded to give me her number,
saying,
"Thank you, for enlightening me,"
and apologized.

I said,
"No worries, love."

Then she giggled and said,
"So, can I join your league?"

I smiled and replied,
"Sure! You're in."
Proverbs 31

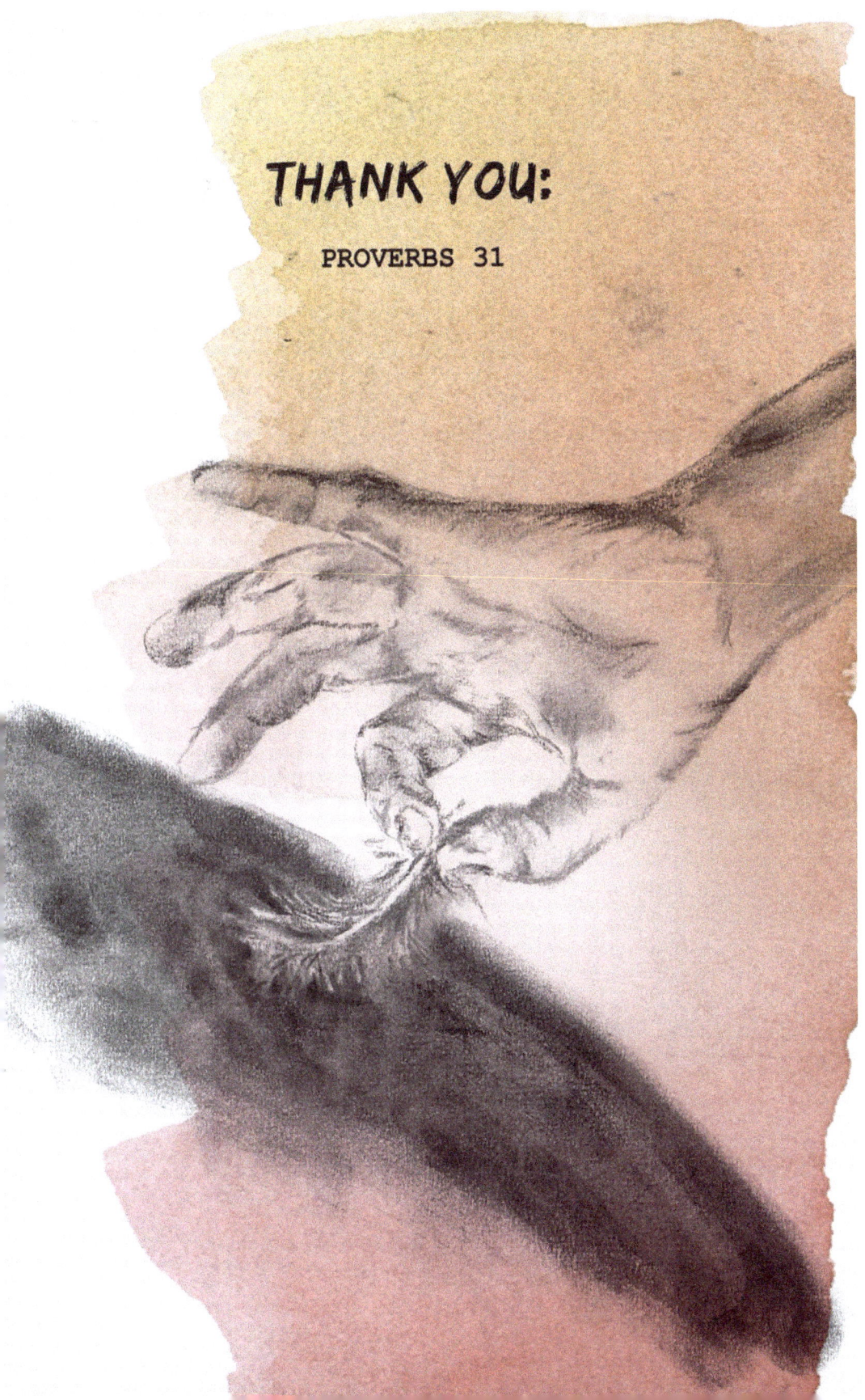

THANK YOU

Thank you for not loving me.
It taught me to love myself.

Thank you for leaving me
and moving on to someone else
(I will pray for them).

Thank you for lying to me,
for scandalizing my name.

We both know you were wrong,
And, for that, you should be ashamed.

I thank you that it taught me
I'm stronger without you,
and even when you didn't believe in self,
I believed in you
(and that right there is a different kind of strength).

So I thank you.
My heart belonged to you, mind, body, and soul.

You promised to love me forever,
that we would stay together till we both grew old
(that was a lie).

FRAGILE, HANDLE WITH CARE.

The late-night phone calls, the mystery texts,
the disrespect, the anger, the lack of sex.

I'm too tired.
It's hot.
Hell, we got air conditioning.

The avoiding me at home,
the silent treatment, not to mention.

I thank you for the attitude,
the going off on me.

It showed me your true colors.
and lack of love for me.

You put everything on me.
I couldn't do right in your eyes.
And while you're sound asleep,
I stayed up and cried.

And after feeling sorry myself,
I would pray over and for you,
putting you before myself
(I thought I was a fool).

I asked for strength to leave you,
to take the love away,

but God is love,
so it's like taking Him away.

I thank you that you ignored me,
limited your time with me,
left me all alone,
but I used my time wisely.

You see,
I cried out to God.
I sought His face
not just His hand.
He said even pain
becomes part of His master plan.

He was growing me,
pruning me, like a flower.
He not only calls me child,
But, now, He calls me daughter.

I thank you.
I was so busy crying over you.
I really lost myself.

I wouldn't even think
about entertaining someone else
(What was I thinking?).

I broke plans with my girls,

avoided their phone calls.
I missed out on brunches, girls' night out and shopping at the mall
(sorry, rain check please).

But hey,
you win some
but also lose some too,

but in the midst of it all, I found me and
I thank you.

Proverbs 31

TOO MUCH SAUCE

PROVERBS 31

FRAGILE, HANDLE WITH CARE.

TOO MUCH SAUCE

The homie, Hot Sauce, was talking to his boy, Tomato Sauce, about ole girl, BBQ Sauce, and her friend, Ms. Ranch Dressing.

How he chilled with both of them on the same night, two hours apart. He took BBQ Sauce to dinner and a movie and tried go in for a night cap, but she wasn't having that. So, he called Ranch Dressing to see what she was doing. Sshe said, "Come over. I'm just watching movies." So, he dipped.

Long story short, he Netflix and chilled with Ms. Ranch Dressing all night.

So, the homie, Tomato Sauce, told his gal, Apple Sauce (SHE SO SWEET), and she told her cousin, Vinaigrette, who told her hairstylist, Blue Cheese, who was kicking it with BBQ Sauce's big brother, ole Sweet and Sour, who was getting his haircut by barber, Chicken Broth.

So, Sweet and Sour confronted Tomato Sauce over the situation about Hot Sauce and his sister, BBQ Sauce. So, he told him everything the homie, Hot Sauce, said, and that made him hotter than boiling water.

A couple of days passed, and the homies, Hot Sauce and Tomato Sauce, were at the park playing basketball when, low and behold, brother Sweet and Sour approached them.

Well ole boy Hot Sauce and....

To be continued...

MORAL: Ladies, make sure you know who you're dealing with beforehand. Some guys are just looking to put another notch in their belt.

Proverbs 31

TORN:

PROVERBS 31

TORN

As much as my body craves to know you intimately,
my heart desires to know you spiritually.

And if given the opportunity,
I would respectfully decline,
for I want not only your body
but also your mind.

Not implying at all that
this will be easy,
but what I want from you is beyond intimacy.

I wanna love you
like Christ loves the church.
I want to shield you from all hurt.
I want to grab your hands
and pray for you in your heartache,

Pray you through,
fall to my knees
and lift you up to the Father,

ask Him how
we can help His lovely daughter.

It's so hard to not want you,

to caress your back,
lay you down ever so gently in my bed,

To experience
what it would feel like
being with you,

but I respect our God
and I respect you too.

I guess I'll be praying for you
the rest of my life,

for I'm not looking just for a girlfriend
but a Godly wife.

So until then,
I guess I'll be. torn
between serving my God
and pleasing my flesh.

The battle continues
(warring against my flesh),
Samuel.

Proverbs 31

WHY ME:
PROVERBS 31

WHY ME

Show me, Father,
what You saw when You first created me.

What exactly did You see
when You had those thoughts of me?

I know that I was created to worship and praise You too,
give You glory where it's due.
You see all that I do
and know, in my heart, I love You.

Where You go,
I will go,
and reverence unto You, I'll bestow.

But often times, I fall short,
never meaning to break Your heart.

I find myself asking why
You call me the Apple of your eye.

With all my mistakes,
You will NEVER leave me nor forsake.

You love me still,
my mess and all,
and when in trouble,

FRAGILE, HANDLE WITH CARE.

on You I call.

You answer me every time,
even when I've crossed the line.

I thank you, Father,
for forgiveness,
for being made strong in my weakness.

I'm not perfect,
I must confess.

Lord, please see me thru this mess.
I'm trying to be all I can be.
I know You love me, but
Why me?

Proverbs 31

BUT I'M WORKING ON IT

PROVERBS 31

BUT I'M WORKING ON IT

Don't get it twisted.
I'm not perfect,
but I'm working on it.

I curse from time to time,
but I'm working on it.

I lust from time to time,
but I'm working on it.

I get mad from time to time,
but I'm working on it.

I indulge in meaningless conversations,
but I'm working on it.

Do things wrong,
but I'm working on it.

Go places I shouldn't ,
but I'm working on it.

Say things I shouldn't,
but I'm working on it.

So don't beat yourself up,
and for sure don't allow

FRAGILE, HANDLE WITH CARE.

anyone else to beat you up about it.

Don't get discouraged.
Keep striving to do and be better.

It's all good
as long as you're working on it.

Greatness is a process.

Proverbs 31

YOU DESERVE IT

You don't have to be spring nor summer time fine.
You are fearfully and wonderfully made,
so your beautiful by design.

A Monet,
a beautiful sunset,
you're truly a work of art.

You don't have to have anything
for you already have my heart.

You were hand crafted by the master,
formed by His hand,
stamped with His approval,
so you need no validation from man.

You were taken from me.
You are my rib.
I'm forever indebted to you for as long as I live.

You've brought me so much joy.
I'll be a fool not to make you my wife.

You don't have to love me
the way you do.
Beautiful mind, so much class,

and sexy too.

So, don't ever let anyone
make you feel like you're not worth it.

You're a queen.
You're royalty and respect.
Yes,
You deserve it.

Proverbs 31